To John

From Mom + Dad

As You Graduate from

Gower Middle School

June 8, 2004

© 2004 by Barbour Publishing, Inc.

ISBN 1-59310-009-4

Cover image © BrandX Pictures

Published by Humble Creek, P.O. Box 719, Uhrichsville, Ohio 44683

Printed in China.
5 4 3 2 1

IN CELEBRATION
OF A NEW DAY

KELLY WILLIAMS

HUMBLECREEK
INSPIRATION FOR LIFE

celebration

Night's
candles are
burnt out,
and jocund
day Stands
tiptoe on
the misty mountaintops.

WILLIAM SHAKESPEARE

Congratulations, graduate!

As you forge out into the world,
a new day is dawning. . . .
Look out into this "new day"
. . .and what do you see?
As the rays of the sun break through
the cover of the morning mist,
the view in the distance becomes clearer.
You see that this new day is one to celebrate. . . .
For on the horizon is a world full of opportunity.
All you must do is reach out and seize it!

Each new day is a gift from God.

Finish each day and be done with it.
You have done what you could;
some blunders and absurdities have crept in;
forget them as soon as you can.
Tomorrow is a new day;
you shall begin it serenely
and with too high a spirit to be
encumbered with your old nonsense.

RALPH WALDO EMERSON

Embrace the wonder and excitement each day brings.

For tomorrow affords us new opportunities. . .

Time to experience. . .

Time to create. . .

Time to reflect. . .

Time to dream.

Dream Big

Shoot for the moon.
Even if you miss,
you'll land among the stars.

LES BROWN

I wish you success on your journey of life.
Always remember to dream. . .and to look
for opportunity in the most unexpected places.

celebration

_May you
always
have stars
within
your reach._

The tragedy of life doesn't lie in not reaching your goal.
The tragedy lies in having no goal to reach.
It isn't a calamity to die with dreams unfilled,
    but it is a calamity not to dream.
It is not disgrace to reach the stars,
    but it is a disgrace to have no stars to reach for.

BENJAMIN MAYS

If you can imagine it, you can achieve it.
If you can dream it, you can become it.

WILLIAM ARTHUR WARD

If one advances confidently in the direction of his dreams
and endeavors to live the life which he has imagined,
he will meet with success unexpected in common hours.

HENRY DAVID THOREAU

Far away there in the sunshine are my highest aspirations.
I may not reach them, but I can look up and see their beauty,
believe in them, and try to follow where they lead.

LOUISA MAY ALCOTT

If you have built castles in the air,
your work need not be lost;
that is where they should be.
Now put the foundations under them.

HENRY DAVID THOREAU

Within our dreams and aspirations
we find our opportunities.

SUE ATCHLEY EBAUGH

Always believe in your dreams.

Boldly take steps to achieve your goals.

Endure all hardships with courage and perseverance.

Look for new opportunities in every day.

Intend to be the best you can be.

Endeavor to live a life God leads.

Venture to go where no one has gone before.

Entrust your future to God.

You see things;

and you say

"Why?"

But I dream things that never were;

and I say

"Why not?"

GEORGE BERNARD SHAW

There is nothing like a dream
to create the future.

VICTOR HUGO

Always dream and shoot higher than you know how to.
Don't bother just to be better than your contemporaries
or predecessors. Try to be better than yourself.

WILLIAM FAULKNER

We grow great by dreams. All big men are dreamers.
They see things in the soft haze of a spring day
or in the red fire of a long winter's evening.
Some of us let these great dreams die,
but others nourish and protect them;
nurse them through bad days till they bring them
to the sunshine and light which comes always to those
who sincerely hope that their dreams will come true.

WOODROW WILSON

Commit yourself to a dream....

Nobody who tries to do something great but fails
is a total failure.
Why? Because he can always rest assured that he
succeeded in life's most important battle—
he defeated the fear of trying.

ROBERT H. SCHULLER

Twenty years from now you will be more disappointed
by the things that you didn't do than by the ones you
did do. So throw off the bowlines. Sail away from the
safe harbor. Catch the trade winds in your sails.

Explore.

Dream.

Discover.

MARK TWAIN

The way I see it, there are two kinds of dreams.

One is a dream that's always going to be just that. . .a dream. . . .
Then there's a dream that's more than a dream; it's like. . .a
map. A map that you live by and follow for the rest of your days
knowing that someday you're going to stand on top of that
mountain holding everything you thought of right there in
your hand!

ROBERT COOPER

Have Faith

The reason birds can fly and we can't is simply
    that they have perfect faith,
for to have faith is to have wings.

                            J. M. BARRIE

As you look forward to the future,
may you always hold fast to your faith.
And remember that, with God,
all things are possible.

Faith is deliberate confidence in the character
of God whose ways you may not understand
at the time.

OSWALD CHAMBERS

Weave in faith, and God will find the thread.

PROVERB

Faith makes the discords of the present the harmonies of
the future.

ROBERT COLLYER

Now faith is being sure of what we hope for
and certain of what we do not see.

HEBREWS 11:1

*Faith consists in believing when
it is beyond the power
of reason to believe.*

VOLTAIRE

18

"If you believe, you will receive whatever you ask for in prayer."

MATTHEW 21:22

Every tomorrow has two handles.
We can take hold of it with the handle of anxiety or
the handle of faith.

HENRY WARD BEECHER

Reason is our soul's left hand,
Faith her right.

JOHN DONNE

19

celebration

As your faith is strengthened
you will find that there is no longer
the need to have a sense of control,
that things will flow as they will,
and that you will flow with them,
to your great delight and benefit.

EMMANUEL TENEY

But if I knew everything,
there would be no wonder,
because what I believe is
far more than I know.

MADELEINE L'ENGLE

"*If you have faith as small as a mustard seed,*
you can say to this mountain,
'Move from here to there'
and it will move.
Nothing will be impossible for you."

MATTHEW 17:20–21

There are many things that are essential to arriving at true peace of mind, and one of the most important is faith, which cannot be acquired without prayer.

JOHN WOODEN

Spend time each day conversing with God. . . and ask Him for the strength and faith you need to meet your failures and your successes head-on.

Persevere

'Tis a lesson you should heed:
    Try, try, try again.
If at first you don't succeed,
    Try, try, try again.

            W. E. HICKSON

God will give you the strength you need to persevere.
Don't be afraid to pick yourself back up and try again.

celebration

A man should conceive of a legitimate purpose in his
  heart and set out to accomplish it. . . .
Even if he fails again and again to accomplish his purpose
  (as he necessarily must until weakness is overcome),
  the strength of character gained will be the measure
  of his true success, and this will form a new
  starting point for future power and triumph.

JAMES ALLEN

*Let us run with perseverance
the race marked out for us.*

HEBREWS 12:1

Great works are performed
not by strength
but by perseverance.

SAMUEL JOHNSON

*For though a righteous man falls
seven times, he rises again.*

PROVERBS 24:16

Develop success from failures.
Discouragement and failure are two of the surest
stepping-stones to success.

DALE CARNEGIE

I am not judged by the number of times I fail,
but by the number of times I succeed;
and the number of times I succeed is in
direct proportion to the number of times
I can fail and keep on trying.

TOM HOPKINS

In the confrontation between the stream and the rock,
the stream always wins—
not through strength but by perseverance.

H. JACKSON BROWN

Genius is divine perseverance.

WOODROW WILSON

All great masters are chiefly distinguished by the power of adding a second, a third, and perhaps a fourth step in a continuous line. Many a man had taken the first step. With every additional step you enhance immensely the value of your first.

RALPH WALDO EMERSON

Success seems to be largely a matter of
hanging on after others have let go.

WILLIAM FEATHER

27

Nothing in this world can take the place of persistence. Talent will not; nothing is more common than unsuccessful men with talent. Genius will not; unrewarded genius is almost a proverb. Education will not; the world is full of educated derelicts. Persistence and determination alone are omnipotent. The slogan "press on" has solved and always will solve the problems of the human race.

CALVIN COOLIDGE

You need to persevere so that when you have done the will of God, you will receive what he has promised.

HEBREWS 10:36

The heights by great men reached and kept
Were not attained by sudden flight,
But they, while their companions slept,
Were toiling upward in the night.

HENRY WADSWORTH LONGFELLOW

All the performances of human art, at which we look with praise or wonder, are instances of the resistless force of perseverance; it is by this that the quarry becomes a pyramid, and that distant countries are united with canals. If a man was to compare the single stroke of the pickaxe, or of one impression of the spade, with the general design and the last result, he would be overwhelmed by the sense of their disproportion; yet those petty operations, incessantly continued, in time surmount the greatest difficulties, and mountains are leveled and oceans bounded by the slender force of human beings.

SAMUEL JOHNSON

Commitment unlocks the doors of imagination,
allows vision, and gives us the "right stuff"
to turn our dreams into reality.

JAMES WOMACK

We consider blessed
those who have persevered.

JAMES 5:11

A Promising Future

With doubt and dismay you are smitten,
You think there's no chance for you, son?
Why the best books haven't been written,
The best race hasn't been run.

BERTON BRALEY

The future belongs to you, grad!
Dream big, have faith, persevere,
and you will succeed.

celebration

The future belongs to those
who believe in the beauty
of their dreams.

ELEANOR ROOSEVELT

When you think all is lost,
the future remains.

ROBERT GODDARD

For I dipt into the future,
   far as human eye could see,
      Saw the Vision of the world
         and all the wonder that would be.

ALFRED, LORD TENNYSON

There is surely a future hope for you.
PROVERBS 23:18

The future is something which everyone reaches
at the rate of sixty minutes an hour,
whatever he does,
whoever he is.

C. S. LEWIS

Take advantage of every tomorrow.
Each day offers twenty-four hours in which we can
either take action and follow our dreams. . .or cave in
when faced with unforeseen challenges.
What will *you* do with tomorrow?

neu

Time is an equal opportunity employer. Each human being has exactly the same number of hours and minutes every day. Rich people can't buy more hours. Scientists can't invent new minutes. And you can't save time to spend it on another day. Even so, time is amazingly fair and forgiving. No matter how much time you've wasted in the past, you still have an entire tomorrow.

DENIS WAITLEY

The best thing about the future is
that it comes only one day at a time.

ABRAHAM LINCOLN

35

celebration

"For I know the plans I have for you,"
declares the LORD,
"plans to prosper you and not to harm you,
plans to give you hope and a future."

JEREMIAH 29:11

*The future is as bright
as the promises of God.*

WILLIAM CAREY

Never be afraid to trust an unknown future to a known God.

CORRIE TEN BOOM

Commit to the LORD whatever you do,
and your plans will succeed.

PROVERBS 16:3

What lies behind us
    and what lies before us
        are tiny matters
            compared to what lies within us.

RALPH WALDO EMERSON

*The future is not
something we enter.
The future is
something we create.*

LEONARD SWEET

neu

Life is no brief candle to me.
It is a sort of splendid torch
which I have got a hold of for the moment,
and I want to make it burn as brightly as possible
before handing it onto future generations.

GEORGE BERNARD SHAW

39

celebration

To dream anything that you want to dream, that is the beauty of the human mind. To do anything that you want to do, that is the strength of the human will. To trust yourself to test your limits, that is the courage to succeed.

BERNARD EDMONDS

Celebrate each new day in your life....
Imagine the possibilities!

Lives of great men all remind us,
We can make our lives sublime,
And, departing, leave behind us,
Footprints on the sands of time.

HENRY WADSWORTH LONGFELLOW